My Bilingual Talking Dictionary

Turkish & English

First published in 2005 by Mantra Lingua
Global House, 303 Ballards Lane, London N12 8NP
www.mantralingua.com

This TalkingPEN edition 2009
Text copyright © 2005 Mantra Lingua
Illustrations copyright © 2005 Mantra Lingua
(except pages 4-9, 42-49 Illustrations copyright © 2005 Priscilla Lamont)
Audio copyright © 2009 Mantra Lingua

With thanks to the illustrators:
David Anstey, Dixie Bedford-Stockwell, Louise Daykin,
Alison Hopkins, Richard Johnson, Allan Jones,
Priscilla Lamont, Yokococo

All rights reserved

A CIP record for this book is available from the British Library

Hear each page of this talking book narrated with the RecorderPEN!
1) To get started touch the arrow button below with the RecorderPEN.
2) To hear the word in English touch the 'E' button at the top of the pages.
3) To hear the word spoken in an English sentence touch the 'S' button at the top of the pages.
4) To hear the language of your choice touch the 'L' button on the top of the pages.
5) Touch the square button below to hear more information about using the Dictionary with the RecorderPEN.

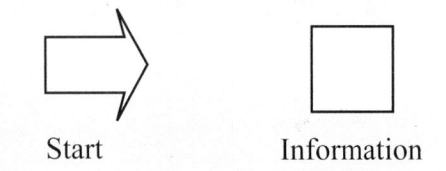

Start   Information

Contents

Kendim
Myself — page 4-5

Kıyafetler
Clothes — page 6-7

Aile
Family — page 8

Ev
Home — page 9

Ev ve içindekiler
House and Contents — page 10-11

Meyve
Fruit — page 12-13

Sebzeler
Vegetables — page 14-15

Yiyecek ve içecek
Food and Drink — page 16-17

Yemek vakti
Meal Time — page 18-19

Şehir
Town — page 20-21

Çarşı
High Street — page 22-23

Yol güvenliği
Road Safety — page 24-25

Taşıma
Transport — page 26-27

Çiftlik hayvanları
Farm Animals — page 28-29

Vahşi hayvanlar
Wild Animals — page 30-31

Deniz kenarı
Seaside — page 32-33

Park
Playground — page 34-35

Sınıf
Classroom — page 36-37

Okul çantası
School Bag — page 38-39

Bilgisayarlar
Computers — page 40-41

Giyinme
Dressing Up — page 42-43

Oyuncaklar ve oyunlar
Toys and Games — page 44-45

Spor
Sport — page 46-47

Müzik
Music — page 48-49

İçindekiler

Uzay
Space — page 50-51

Hava durumu
Weather — page 52-53

Yılın ayları
Months of the Year — page 54

Mevsimler
Seasons — page 54

Haftanın günleri
Days of the Week — page 55

Zamanı söylemek
Telling the Time — page 55

Renkler
Colours — page 56

Şekiller
Shapes — page 56

Sayılar 1-20
Numbers 1-20 — page 57

Karşıtlar
Opposites — page 58-59

İndeks
Index — page 60-64

Myself

gözler
goezler
eyes

saç
such
hair

ağız
aa-uz
mouth

kulaklar
koo-luck-lar
ears

dişler
dish-lér
teeth

el
elle
hand

baş parmak
bash-pur-muk
thumb

kol bileği
coal bee-leyee
wrist

parmaklar
pur-muk-lar
fingers

bel
belle
waist

ayak
a-yuck
feet

ayak parmakları
a-yuck pur-muk-lareh
toes

---

mutlu
moot-loo
happy

üzgün
uz-gun
sad

kızgın
kez-gen
angry

kıskanç
kes-kunch
jealous

heyecanlı
hé-yé-jun-leh
excited

4

Kendim

yüz
yiuz
face

kafa
ka-fa
head

burun
boo-roon
nose

boyun
bo-yoon
neck

kol
coal
arm

omuzlar
o-mooz-lar
shoulders

karın
ka-ren
stomach

dirsek
dir-séck
elbow

diz
deez
knee

sırt
sert
back

ayak bileği
a-yuck bee-leyee
ankle

bacak
ba-juck
leg

hasta
hus-tuh
sick

aç
ach
hungry

korkmuş
cork-moosh
scared

çekingen
ché-keen-gén
shy

yorgun
your-goon
tired

5

Clothes

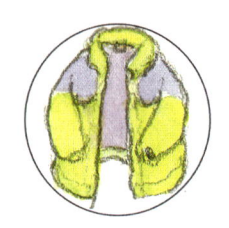

palto
pal-to
coat

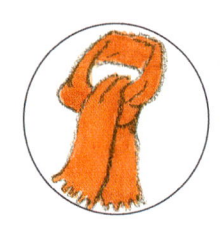

kaşkol
cush-coal
scarf

tişört
t-shirt
t-shirt

elbise
élle-bee-sé
dress

etek
é-ték
skirt

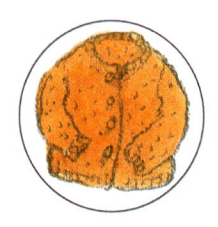

hırka
her-kaa
cardigan

mayo
maa-yo
swimming costume

kilotlu çorap
kee-lot-loo cho-rup
tights

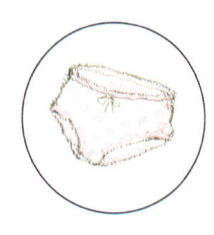

külot
kee-lot
knickers

ayakkabı
aa-yuck-kaa-beh
shoes

Kıyafetler

eldiven
elle-dee-ven
gloves

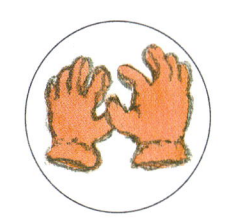

şapka
shup-kaa
hat

gömlek
goem-lék
shirt

kazak
kaa-zuck
jumper

pantolon
pan-to-lon
trousers

şort
şort
shorts

mayo
maa-yo
swimming trunks

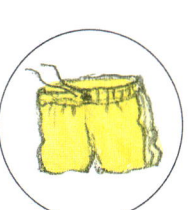

çorap
cho-rup
socks

don
don
underpants

spor ayakkabısı
spor aa-yuck-kaa-beh-seh
trainers

Family

Aile

babaanne
ba-baa-an-né
grandmother

büyükbaba
biu-yiuk ba-ba
grandfather

dede
dede
grandfather

anneanne
an-né-an-né
grandmother

hala
ha-la
aunt

baba
ba-ba
father

anne
an-né
mother

dayı
daa-yeh
uncle

erkek kardeş
ér-kék kar-désh
brother

kız kardeş
kehz kar-désh
sister

oğul
o-ool
son

kız
kehz
daughter

bebek
bé-bék
baby

Home Ev

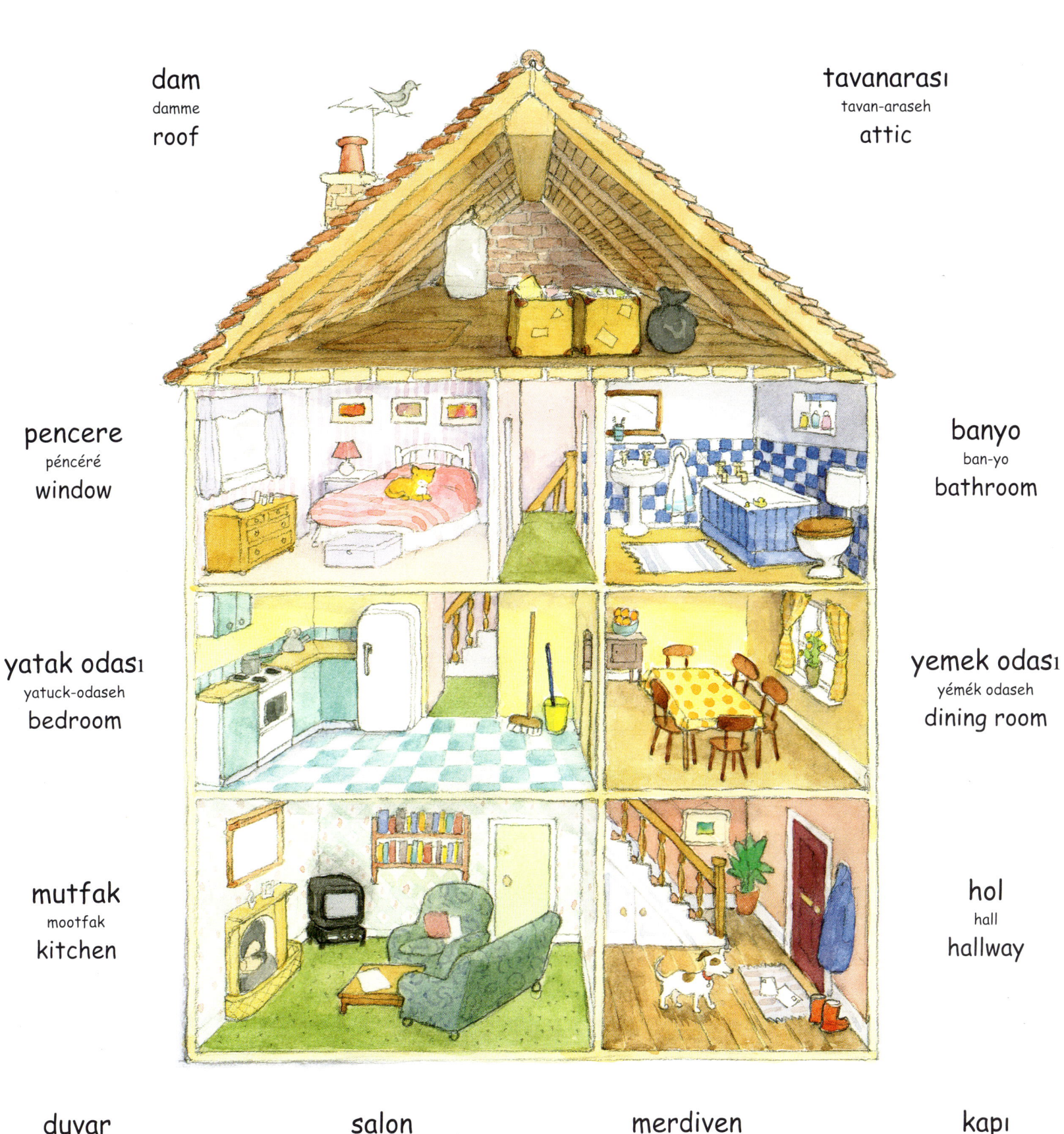

dam
damme
roof

tavanarası
tavan-araseh
attic

pencere
péncéré
window

banyo
ban-yo
bathroom

yatak odası
yatuck-odaseh
bedroom

yemek odası
yémék odaseh
dining room

mutfak
mootfak
kitchen

hol
hall
hallway

duvar
doo-var
wall

salon
salone
lounge/living room

merdiven
mérdivén
staircase

kapı
kapeh
door

9

House and Contents

yastık
yastick
pillow

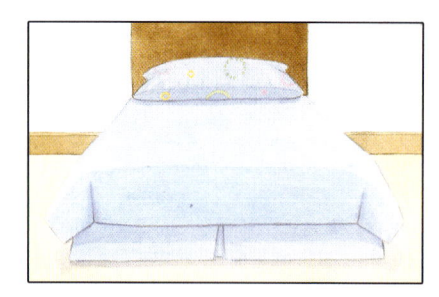

yatak
yatuck
bed

yorgan
yourgun
blanket

çöp kutusu
choep kootoosoo
bin

vantilatör
vantilateur
fan

lamba
lumba
lamp

telefon
telephone
telephone

çamaşır makinesi
chamasher makinési
washing machine

ekmek kızartıcısı
ékmék kehzartehjehseh
toaster

su ısıtıcısı
soo ehsehtehjehseh
kettle

çeşme
chéshmé
tap

buzdolabı
boozdolabeh
fridge

ocak
ojuck
cooker

lavabo
lavabeau
sink

10

Ev ve içindekiler

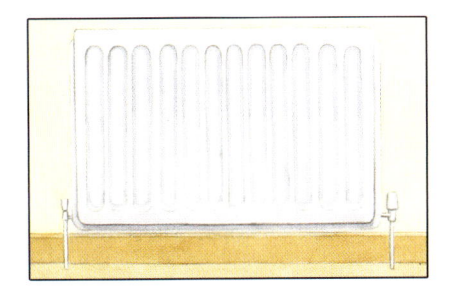

kalorifer
kalorifér
radiator

küvet
kiuvét
bath

havlu
huvloo
towel

ayna
ayna
mirror

tuvalet
toovalét
toilet

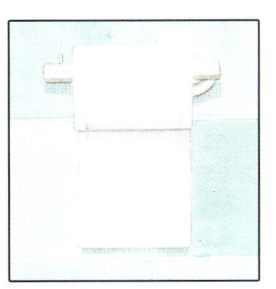

tuvalet kağıdı
toovalét kaideh
toilet roll

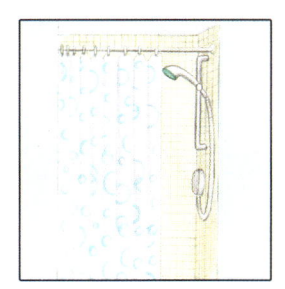

duş
douche
shower

televizyon
télévizyon
television

radyo
rad-yo
radio

perde
pérdé
curtains

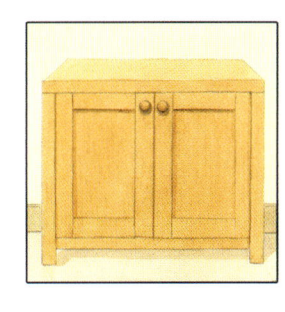

dolap
dolap
cupboard

halı
haleh
carpet

kanape
canapé
sofa

masa
musuh
table

11

Fruit

muz
mooz
banana

papaya
papaya
papaya

armut
armoot
pear

kavun
kaavoon
melon

erik
érik
plum

limon
leemon
lemon

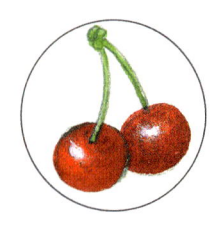

kiraz
keyraz
cherries

çilek
chilek
strawberries

Meyve

üzüm
iuzium
grapes

ananas
ananas
pineapple

mango
mango
mango

portakal
por-takall
orange

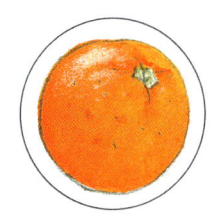

şeftali
sheftalee
peach

elma
élma
apple

liçi
lychee
lychees

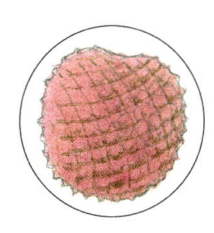

nar
nar
pomegranate

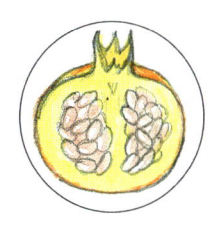

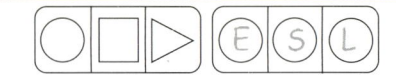

Vegetables

soğan
saw-un
onion

karnıbahar
curnibahar
cauliflower

patates
patatés
potato

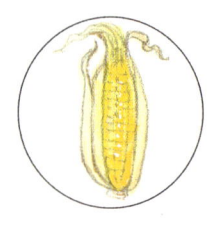

mısır
mehsehr
sweetcorn

mantar
muntur
mushroom

domates
doe-matés
tomato

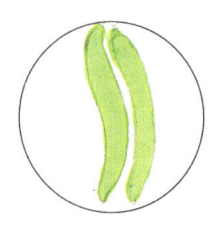

fasulye
fusoolyé
beans

turp
toorp
radish

Sebzeler

sarımsak
saruhmsuck
garlic

kabak
kubuck
pumpkin/squash

salatalık
sala-taluck
cucumber

brokoli
broccoli
broccoli

biber
beebér
pepper/capsicum

havuç
havooch
carrot

marul
marule
lettuce

bezelye
bézélyé
peas

15

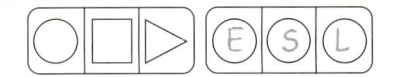

Food and Drink

ekmek ékmék bread	**tereyağı** téréyaaeh butter	**reçel** réchél jam	**sandviç** sandwich sandwich
şeker shékér sugar	**bal** baal honey	**tahıl** tahil cereal	**süt** siout milk
erişte éreeshté noodles	**pilav** peelove rice	**spagetti/makarna** spaghetti/makarna spaghetti	**pizza** pizza pizza
et ét meat	**balık** buluck fish	**yumurta** yoomoorta egg	**peynir** péyneer cheese

16

Yiyecek ve içecek

çikolata
cheekolata
chocolate

şeker
shékér
sweets

pasta
pasta
cake

tatlı
tatleh
pudding

yoğurt
yo-urt
yoghurt

dondurma
don-doormah
ice cream

bisküi
bis-kwee
biscuit

cips
jips
crisps

kızarmış patates
kehzarmehsh patatés
chips

ketçap
ketchup
ketchup

hardal
hur-duhl
mustard

çorba
chorbah
soup

meyve suyu
méyvé sooyoo
fruit juice

maden suyu
madén sooyoo
mineral water

tuz
tooz
salt

biber
beebér
pepper

17

Meal Time

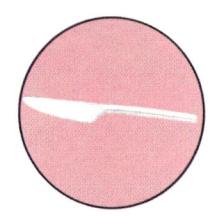

bıçak
behchuck
knife

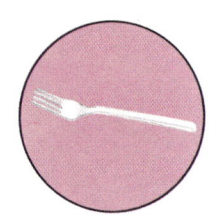

çatal
chatal
fork

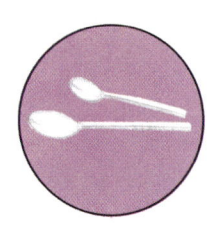

kaşık
kuhshuck
spoon

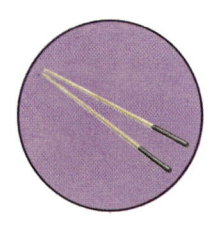

çop stik
chop stick
chopsticks

fincan
feenjun
mug

fincan
feenjuneh
cup

bardak
barduck
glass

18

Yemek vakti

tabak
tubuck
plate

kase
kyasé
bowl

tencere
ténjéré
saucepan

vok
wok
wok

tava
tuvuh
frying pan

termos
thermos
flask

yemek sepeti
yémék sépétee
lunchbox

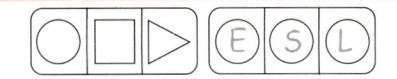

Town

süpermarket
supermarket
supermarket

otopark
autopark
car park

spor merkezi
spor mérkézee
sports centre

kütüphane
kiutiuphané
library

karakol
caracoal
police station

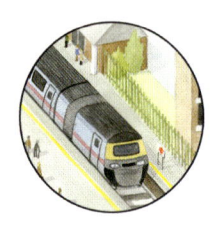

gar
gar
train station

itfaiye
eetfayeh
fire station

Şehir

hastane
hustané
hospital

park
park
park

sinema
cinema
cinema

garaj
garage
garage

otobüs durağı
autobius dooraeh
bus station

dükkânlar
diukyanlaar
shops/stores

okul
ocool
school

21

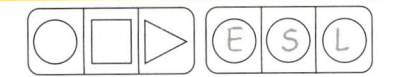

High Street

restoran
restauran
restaurant

çiçekçi
cheechékchee
florist

gazeteci
gazéttéjee
newspaper stand

kitapçı
keetapcheh
book shop

kasap
kasup
butcher

posthane
posthané
post office

balıkçı
baklukjeh
fishmonger

Çarşı

manav
munuv
greengrocer

eczane
éjzané
chemist

fırın
furun
bakery

banka
banka
bank

oyuncak dükkânı
Oioonjakch diukaneh
toyshop

kafe
café
coffee shop

kuaför
coiffeur
hairdressers

23

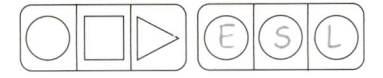

Road Safety

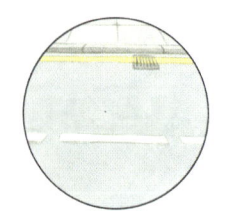

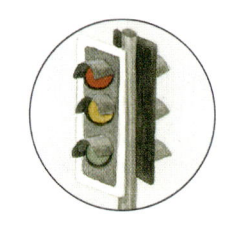

yol
yol
road

trafik ışıkları
traffic ehsheklareh
traffic light

kırmızı ışık
kehrmehzeh ehshehk
red man

yeşil ışık
yéshil yaya ehshehk
green man

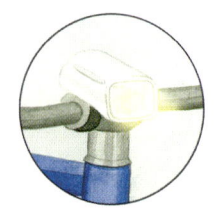

ışıklar
ehshucklaar
lights

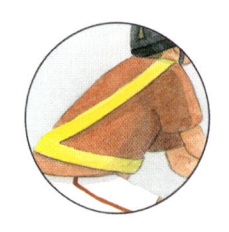

reflektör
reflecteor
reflector

bisiklet kaskı
beeseeklet kusckeh
cycle helmet

yaya geçidi
yaya gecheedee
pedestrian crossing

Yol güvenliği

yürü
yiuriu
go

dur
duur
stop

bak
buck
look

dinle
deanlé
listen

çocuk geçidi
chojook gecheedee
children crossing

okul geçidi trafik polisi
okool gecheedee traffic poleesee
school crossing patrol officer

emiyet kemeri
émneeyét kéméree
seat belt

kaldırım
kuldurum
pavement

25

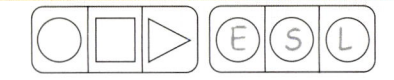

Transport

uçak
oochuck
aeroplane

kamyon
come-yon
lorry/truck

araba
araba
car

otobüs
autobius
coach

vapur
vapour
boat

bisiklet
beeseeklet
bicycle

tren
tren
train

Taşıma

motosiklet
motoseeklét
motorbike

helikopter
helicopter
helicopter

otobüs
autobius
bus

tramvay
tramvay
tram

karavan
caravan
caravan

gemi
gémee
ship

rikşo
rickshaw
rickshaw

27

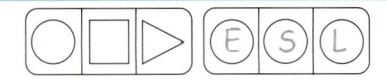

Farm Animals

kuş
koosh
bird

at
at
horse

ördek
oerdék
duck

kedi
kédee
cat

keçi
kéchee
goat

tavşan
tuvshun
rabbit

tilki
teelkee
fox

Çiftlik hayvanları

inek
eeneck
cow

köpek
koepek
dog

koyun
koyoon
sheep

fare
faré
mouse

tavuk
taavook
hen

eşek
ésh-shék
donkey

kaz
cuz
goose

29

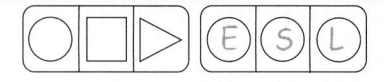

Wild Animals

maymun
my-moon
monkey

fil
fille
elephant

yılan
yehlun
snake

zebra
zébra
zebra

aslan
aslan
lion

su aygırı
soo aygehreh
hippopotamus

yunus
yoonoos
dolphin

balina
baleena
whale

Vahşi hayvanlar

panda
panda
panda bear

zürafa
ziurafaa
giraffe

deve
dévé
camel

kaplan
cup-lunn
tiger

ayı
ayeh
bear

penguen
pénguén
penguin

timsah
timsah
crocodile

köpek balığı
koepek baleheh
shark

31

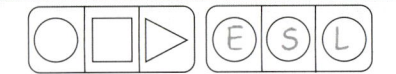

Seaside

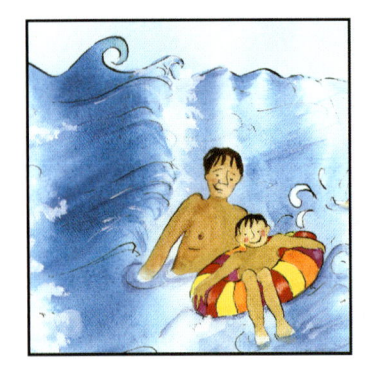

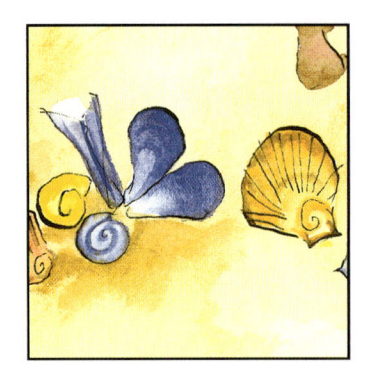

deniz	dalgalar	sahil	cankurtaran
déniz	dahlgahlar	saheel	jun-koortaran
sea	waves	beach	lifeguard

güneş yağı	istridye kabuğu	çakıl taşları	yosun
giunesh yaeh	eestreedyé kaboouh	chuckehl tashlareh	yosoon
sun lotion	shells	pebbles	seaweed

Deniz kenarı

kaya havuzu
kaya havoozoo
rock pool

yengeç
yéngéch
crab

deniz yıldızı
déniz yehldehzeh
starfish

şezlong
chaise-longue
deckchair

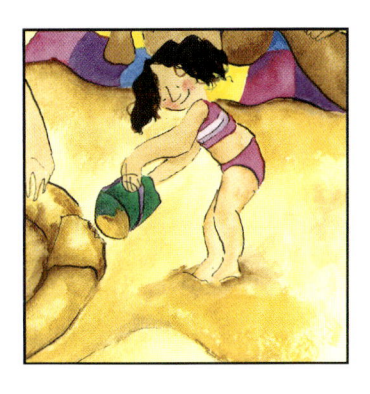

kum
koom
sand

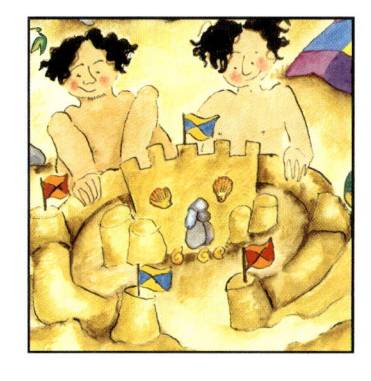

kumdan kale
koomdun callais
sandcastle

kova
ko-va
bucket

kürek
kiu-wreck
spade

33

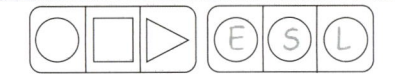

Playground

salıncak
salehnjuck
swing

dönme dolap
deonmé dolup
roundabout

tahterevalli
tuh-tir-e-valley
seesaw

kum havuzu
kum havoosooh
sandpit

tünel
tiunel
tunnel

içinde
eecheendé
in

dışında
dushundah
out

sekmek
sékmék
skip

34

Park

tırmanma çerçevesi
tehrmanmah chérchévésee
climbing frame

yukarı
yookareh
up

kaydırak
kaydehruck
slide

aşağı
ashaeh
down

üstten
uisttén
over

alttan
alttan
under

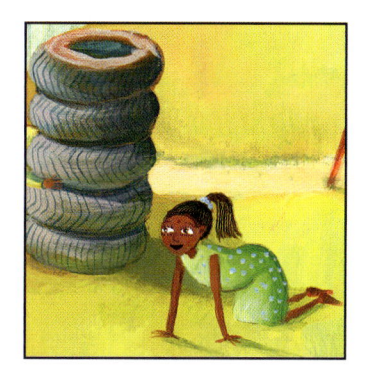

önünde
oeniundé
in front

arkasında
arc-a-sehndah
behind

35

… ESL

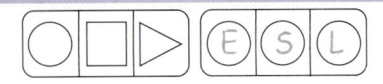

The Classroom

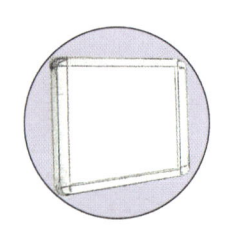

beyaz tahta
béyaz tahta
white board

karatahta
kara tahta
chalk board

sıra
sehrah
desk

sandalye
sandalyé
chair

takvim
tuckveem
calendar

kaset çalar
cassette chalar
tape recorder

kaset
casette
cassette tape

hesap makinesi
hésup makinésee
calculator

Sınıf

öğretmen
eoyretmen
teacher

kitaplar
keetuplar
books

kağıt
keyut
paper

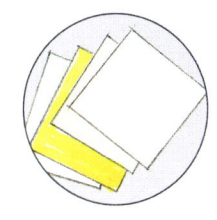

boya
boyaa
paint

boyama fırçası
boyama fehrchaseh
paintbrush

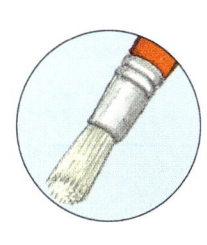

makas
muckus
scissors

tutkal
tootkal
glue

seloteyp
sélotape
sticky tape

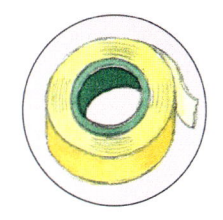

37

School Bag

defter
déftér
writing book

matematik kitabı
matématik keetabeh
maths book

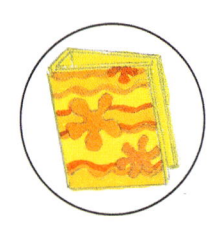

dosya
dosyuh
folder

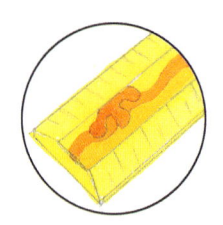

cetvel
jetvel
ruler

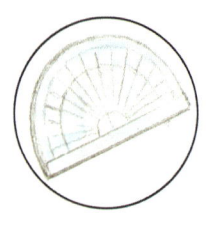

açı ölçer
achuh oelcher
protractor

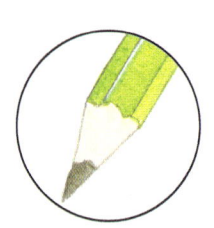

kalem
kalém
pencil

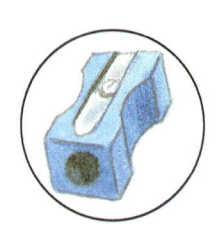

kalem traş
kalém trash
pencil sharpener

Okul çantası

kitap
keetup
reading book

mumlu boya
moomloo boya
crayon

ip
eep
string

para
paraa
money

pusula
pusula
compass

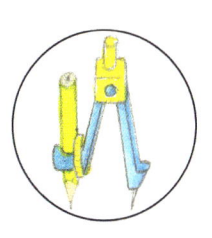

silgi
seelgee
rubber/eraser

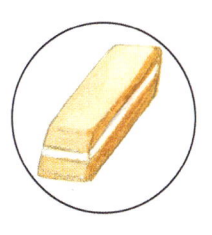

gazlı kalem
gazleh kalem
felt tip pen

39

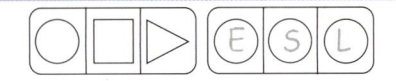

Computers

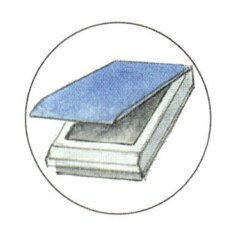

tarayıcı
tarayehjeh
scanner

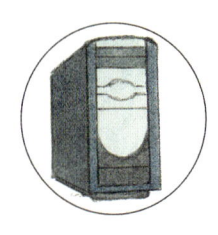

bilgisayar
beelgeesayar
computer

ekran
ékrun
monitor

klavye
clavier
keyboard

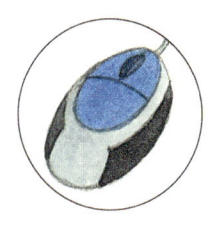

fare
faré
mouse

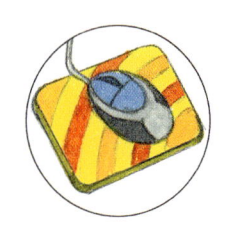

fare altlığı
faré altleegee
mouse mat

Bilgisayarlar

yazıcı
yazehjeh
printer

ekran
ékrun
screen

internet
internet
internet

e-mail
é-mail
email

cd
cd
cd disc

disket
diskette
floppy disc

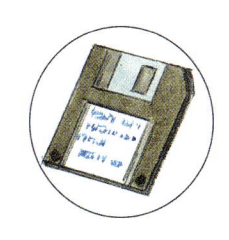

41

Dressing Up

astronot
astronaut
astronaut

polis memuru
police mémooroo
police person

veteriner
vétérinér
vet

itfaiyeci
eetfayéci
firefighter

ressam
réssum
artist

dükkân sahibi
duekkan sahibi
shop keeper

jokey
joké
jockey

kovboy
cowboy
cowboy

ahçı
ahcheh
chef

42

Giyinme

hemşire
hémsheeré
nurse

araba tamircisi
arabuh tameerjeesee
mechanic

tren sürücüsü
tren siuriujiusiu
train driver

balerina
ballerina
ballet dancer

pop yıldızı
pop yehldehzeh
pop star

palyaço
palyacho
clown

korsan
korsun
pirate

büyücü
biuyiujiu
wizard

doktor
doctor
doctor

43

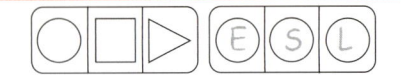

Toys and Games

balon
balon
balloon

boncuklar
bonjooklar
beads

oyun
oyoon
board game

oyuncak bebek
oyoonjuck bébék
doll

oyuncak bebek evi
oyoonjuck bébék evee
doll's house

uçurtma
oochoortmuh
kite

çözmece/bilmece
chiozmeje/bilmeje
puzzle

atlama ipi
atlumuh eepee
skipping rope

topaç
topuch
spinning top

44

Oyuncaklar ve oyunlar

lego
lego
building blocks

satranç
sutrunch
chess

zar
zaar
dice

misketler
meesketler
marbles

oyun kartları
oyoon kartlareh
playing cards

kukla
kookluh
puppet

oyuncak ayı
oyoonjuck ayeh
teddy bear

tren seti
tren setee
train set

oyuncak araba
oyoonjuck arabah
toy car

45

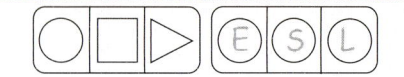

Sport

basketbol
basketball
basketball

top
top
ball

kriket
cricket
cricket

badminton
badminton
badminton

yüzmek
yiuzmeck
swimming

paten
patén
roller skates

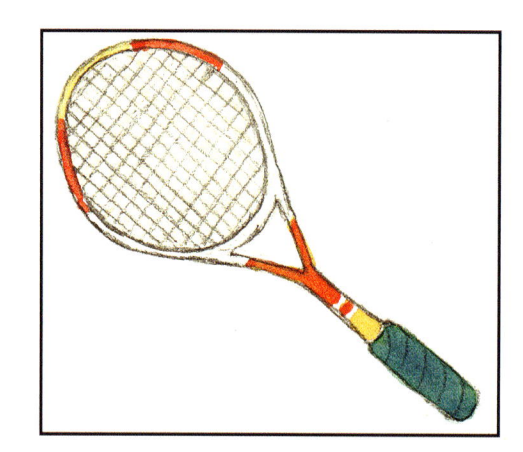

raket
racquet
racquet

buz pateni
booz paténee
ice skates

46

Spor

tenis
tennis
tennis

sopa
sopa
bat

netbol
netball
netball

futbol
football
football

bisiklet sürmek
beeseeklét siurmeck
cycling

ragbi
rugby
rugby

kaykay
kai-kai
skateboard

hoki
hokey
hockey

47

Music

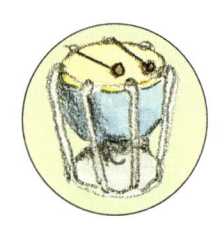

davul
davool
drum

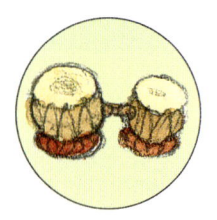

tabla
tabla
tabla

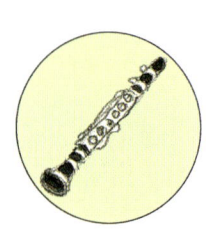

klarinet
clarinet
clarinet

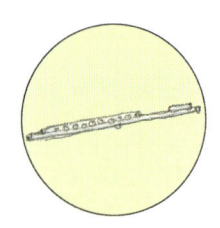

flüt
flute
flute

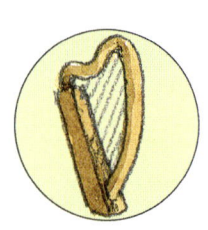

arp
arp
harp

müzik klavyesi
muezik kla-vaysi
keyboard

gitar
guitar
guitar

nota sehpası
nota sehpaseh
music stand

48

Müzik

müzik üçgeni
muezik uichkénee
musical triangle

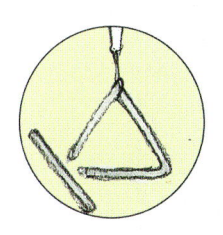

trompet
trumpet
trumpet

maraka
maraca
maracas

gan gan
gan gan
gan gan

piyano
piano
piano

blok flüt
block flute
recorder

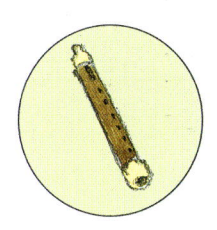

keman
kéman
violin

zaylafon
zaylafon
xylophone

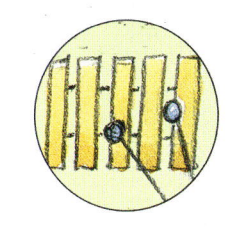

49

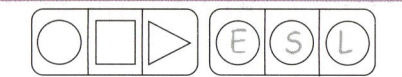

Space

güneş
guinésh
sun

Merkür
merkuir
Mercury

Venüs
venuis
Venus

Dünya
duinyaa
Earth

ay
ay
moon

uzay gemisi
oozay gémeesee
spaceship

kayan yıldız
kayan yehldehz
shooting star

roket
roket
rocket

50

Uzay

Mars
mars
Mars

Jüpiter
jupitér
Jupiter

Satürn
satuirn
Saturn

Üranüs
uiranuis
Uranus

kuyruklu yıldız
kooyrookloo yehldehz
comet

yıldızlar
yehldehzlar
stars

Neptün
neptuin
Neptune

Pluto
pluto
Pluto

51

Weather

güneşli
guineshlee
sunny

gökkuşağı
goek-kooshaeh
rainbow

yağmurlu
yaamoorloo
rainy

gök gürültüsü
goek guiruiltuisui
thunder

şimşek
sheemshék
lightning

fırtınalı
fehrtehnaaleh
stormy

Hava durumu

rüzgarlı
ruizgyarleh
windy

sisli
seeslee
foggy

karlı
karleh
snowy

bulutlu
boolootloo
cloudy

dolu
doloo
hail

buzlu
boosloo
icy

53

Months of the Year

Yılın ayları

ocak
ojuck
January

şubat
shoebut
February

mart
mart
March

nisan
nissan
April

mayıs
my-ehs
May

haziran
hazeerun
June

temmuz
témmooz
July

ağustos
aoustos
August

eylül
éyluil
September

ekim
ékeem
October

kasım
kasehm
November

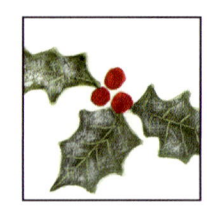

aralık
aralehk
December

Seasons

Mevsimler

ilk bahar
eelk bahar
Spring

yaz
yaz
Summer

son bahar
son bahar
Autumn/Fall

kış
kehsh
Winter

muson
monsoon
Monsoon

54

Days of the Week

Haftanın günleri

pazartesi
pazartésee
Monday

salı
saleh
Tuesday

çarşamba
charshambah
Wednesday

perşembe
pershembeh
Thursday

cuma
jooma
Friday

cumartesi
joomartésee
Saturday

pazar
pazar
Sunday

Telling the Time

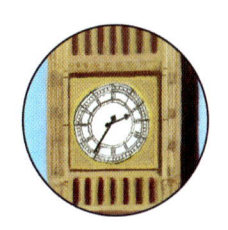

Zamanı söylemek

saat
saat
clock

gün
guin
day

gece
géjé
night

sabah
sabah
morning

akşam
ackshum
evening

kol saati
coal saatee
watch

çeyrek geçe
cheyreck géché
quarter past

buçuk
boochook
half past

çeyrek var
cheyreck var
quarter to

55

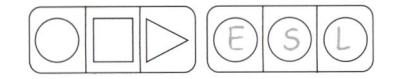

Colours — Renkler

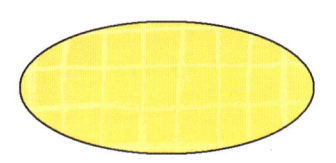

kırmızı
kehrmehzeh
red

turuncu
tooroonkoo
orange

sarı
sareh
yellow

yeşil
yesheel
green

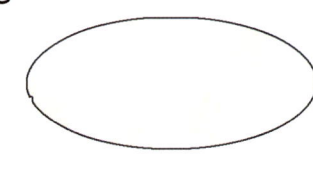

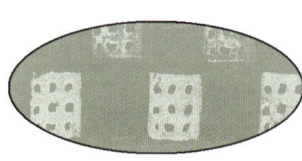

siyah
seeyah
black

beyaz
béyaz
white

gri
gree
grey

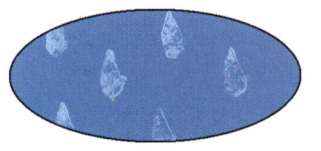

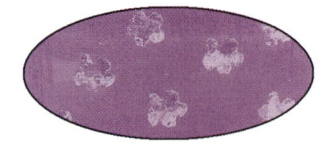

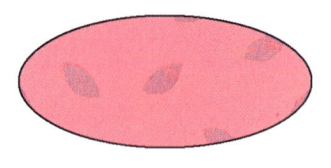

mavi
mavee
blue

mor
more
purple

pembe
pémbé
pink

kahve rengi
kahvé réngee
brown

Shapes — Şekiller

çember
chémbér
circle

yıldız
yehldehz
star

üçgen
uichgén
triangle

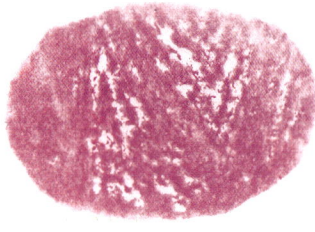

oval
oval
oval

koni
conee
cone

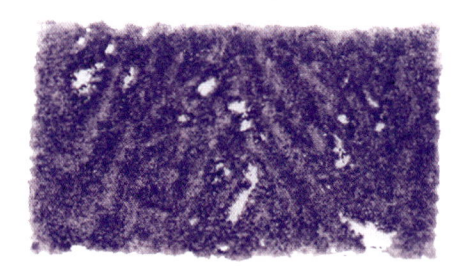

dikdörtgen
deek doertgén
rectangle

kare
Ka-reh
square

56

Numbers 1-20

Sayılar 1-20

	1	**bir** beer one		11	**onbir** on beer eleven
	2	**iki** eekee two		12	**oniki** on eekee twelve
	3	**üç** uich three		13	**onüç** on uich thirteen
	4	**dört** doert four		14	**ondört** on doert fourteen
	5	**beş** bésh five		15	**onbeş** on bésh fifteen
	6	**altı** alteh six		16	**onaltı** on alteh sixteen
	7	**yedi** yédee seven		17	**onyedi** on yédee seventeen
	8	**sekiz** sekeez eight		18	**onsekiz** on sekeez eighteen
	9	**dokuz** dokooz nine		19	**ondokuz** on dokooz nineteen
	10	**on** on ten		20	**yirmi** yeermee twenty

57

Opposites

hızlı
hehzleh
fast

yavaş
yuvush
slow

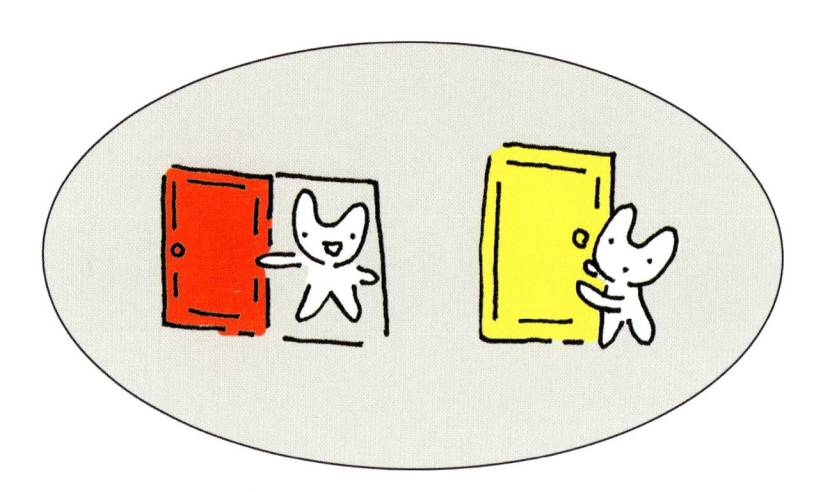

açık
achehk
open

kapalı
kapaleh
closed

büyük
buiyuik
large

küçük
kuichuik
small

ıslak
ehsluck
wet

kuru
kooroo
dry

sıcak
sehjuck
hot

soğuk
so-oock
cold

tatlı
tatleh
sweet

ekşi
ékshee
sour

58

Karşıtlar

yakın
yakehn
near

uzak
oozuck
far

sol
sol
left

sağ
saa
right

ön
oen
front

arka
arka
back

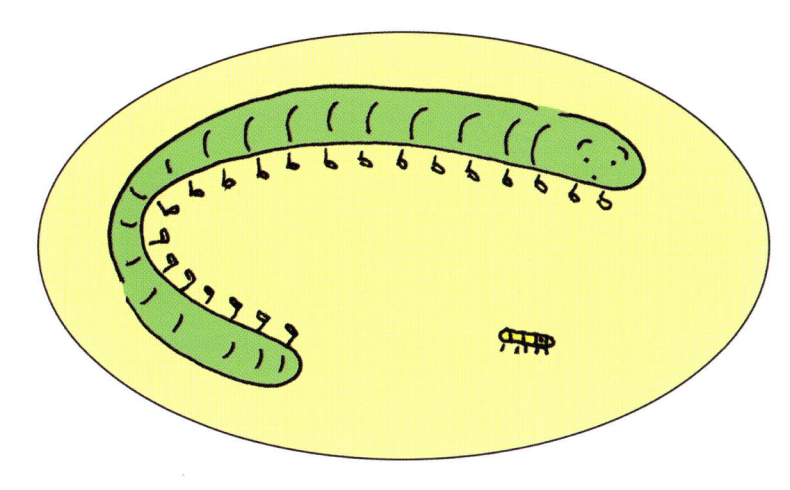

uzun
oozoon
long

kısa
kehsah
short

ağır
aaehr
heavy

hafif
hafeef
light

boş
bosh
empty

dolu
doloo
full

59

Index

Search for a word by picture or by the English word

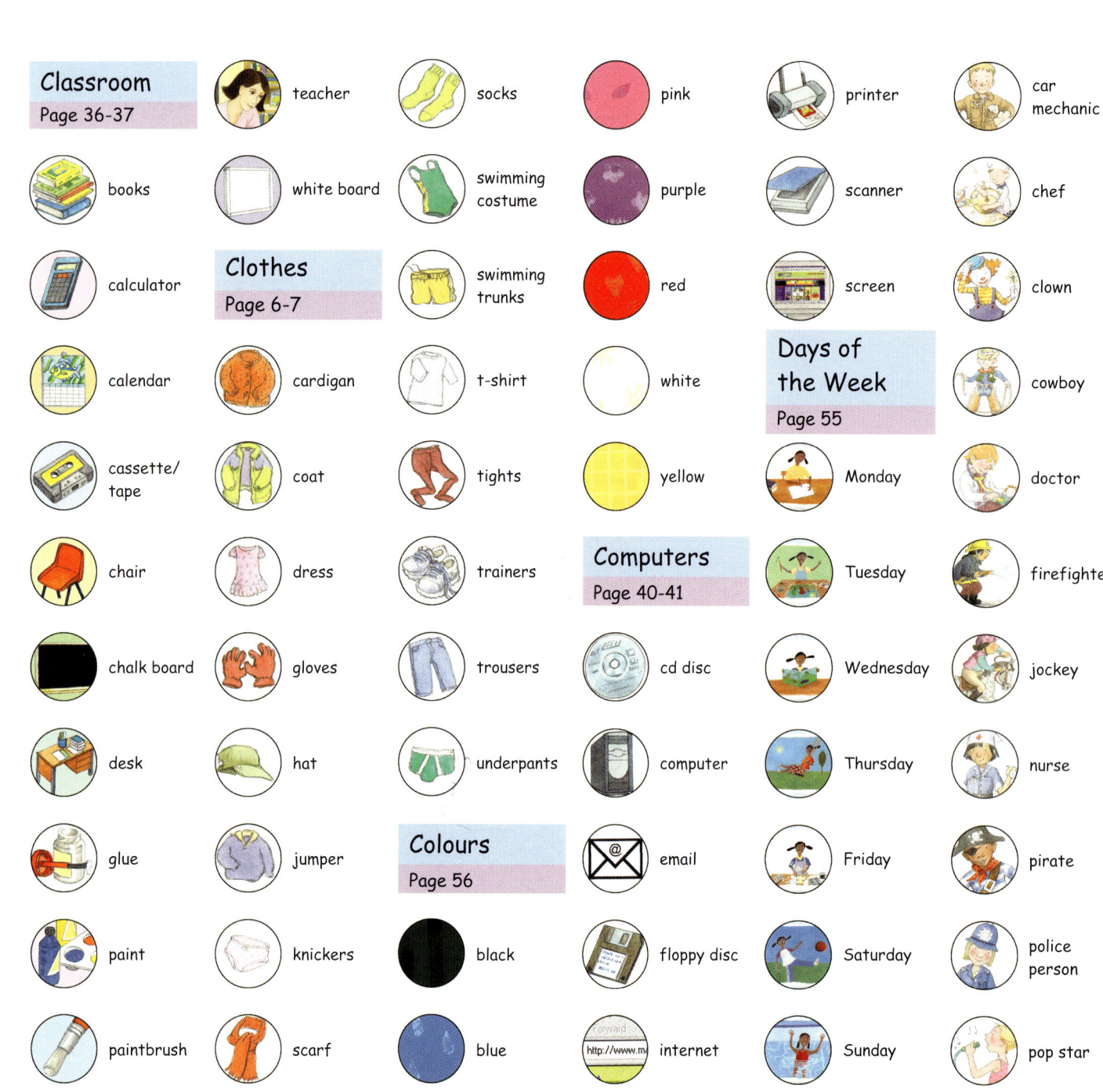

Classroom Page 36-37	teacher	socks	pink	printer	car mechanic	**Family** Page 8
books	white board	swimming costume	purple	scanner	chef	aunt
calculator	**Clothes** Page 6-7	swimming trunks	red	screen	clown	baby
calendar	cardigan	t-shirt	white	**Days of the Week** Page 55	cowboy	brother
cassette/ tape	coat	tights	yellow	Monday	doctor	daughter
chair	dress	trainers	**Computers** Page 40-41	Tuesday	firefighter	father
chalk board	gloves	trousers	cd disc	Wednesday	jockey	grandfather
desk	hat	underpants	computer	Thursday	nurse	grandmother
glue	jumper	**Colours** Page 56	email	Friday	pirate	mother
paint	knickers	black	floppy disc	Saturday	police person	sister
paintbrush	scarf	blue	internet	Sunday	pop star	son
paper	shirt	brown	keyboard	**Dressing Up** Page 42-43	shop keeper	uncle
scissors	shoes	green	monitor	artist	train driver	**Farm Animals** Page 28-29
sticky tape	shorts	grey	mouse	astronaut	vet	bird
tape recorder	skirt	orange	mouse mat	ballet dancer	wizard	cat

60

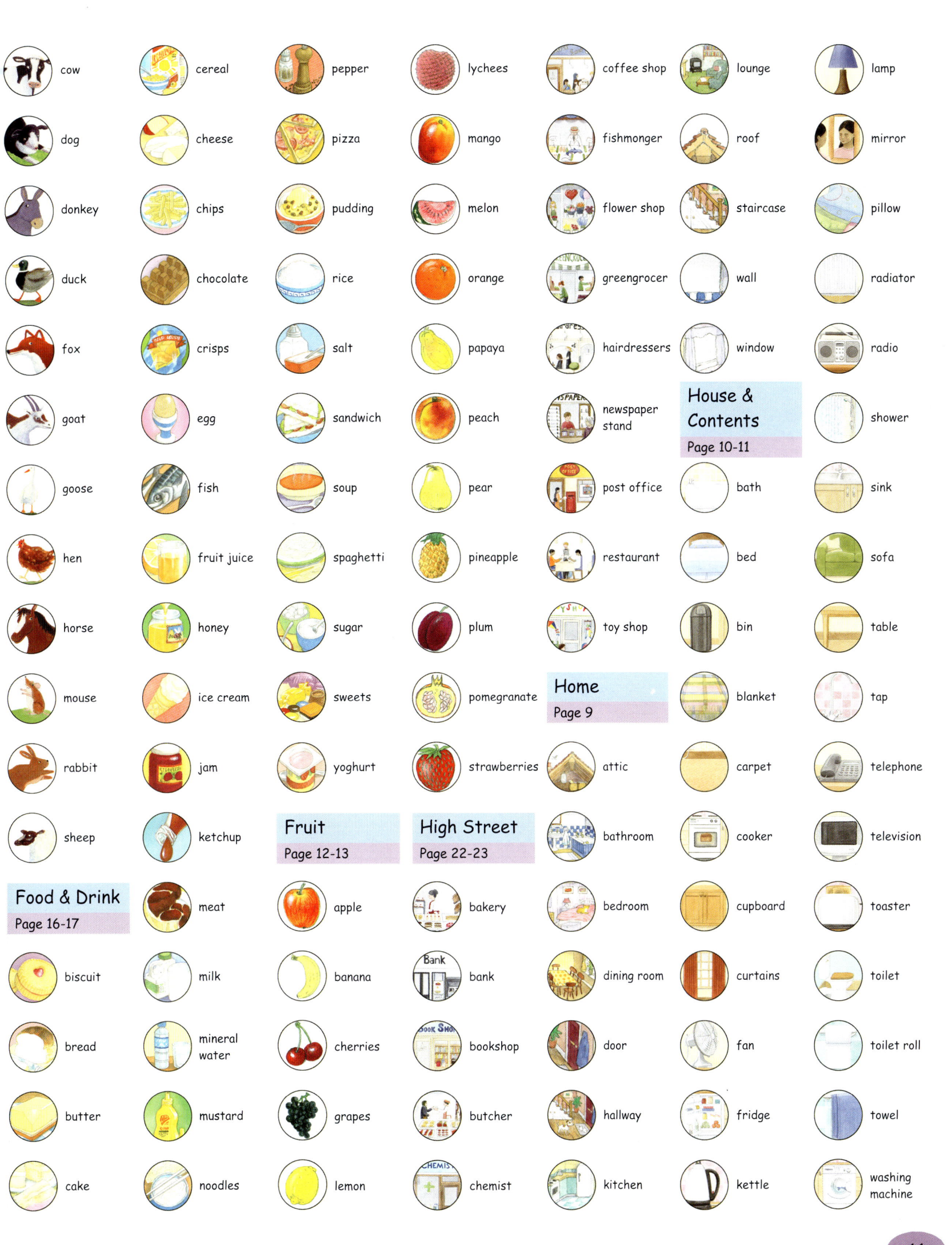

cow	cereal	pepper	lychees	coffee shop	lounge	lamp
dog	cheese	pizza	mango	fishmonger	roof	mirror
donkey	chips	pudding	melon	flower shop	staircase	pillow
duck	chocolate	rice	orange	greengrocer	wall	radiator
fox	crisps	salt	papaya	hairdressers	window	radio
goat	egg	sandwich	peach	newspaper stand	**House & Contents** Page 10-11	shower
goose	fish	soup	pear	post office	bath	sink
hen	fruit juice	spaghetti	pineapple	restaurant	bed	sofa
horse	honey	sugar	plum	toy shop	bin	table
mouse	ice cream	sweets	pomegranate	**Home** Page 9	blanket	tap
rabbit	jam	yoghurt	strawberries	attic	carpet	telephone
sheep	ketchup	**Fruit** Page 12-13	**High Street** Page 22-23	bathroom	cooker	television
Food & Drink Page 16-17	meat	apple	bakery	bedroom	cupboard	toaster
biscuit	milk	banana	bank	dining room	curtains	toilet
bread	mineral water	cherries	bookshop	door	fan	toilet roll
butter	mustard	grapes	butcher	hallway	fridge	towel
cake	noodles	lemon	chemist	kitchen	kettle	washing machine

61

Meal Time
Page 18-19

- bowl
- chopsticks
- cup
- flask
- fork
- frying pan
- glass
- knife
- lunchbox
- mug
- plate
- saucepan
- spoon
- wok

Months of the Year
Page 54

- January
- February
- March
- April
- May
- June
- July
- August
- September
- October
- November
- December

Music
Page 48-49

- clarinet
- drum
- flute
- gan gan
- guitar
- harp
- keyboard
- maracas
- musical triangle
- music stand
- piano
- recorder
- tabla
- trumpet
- violin
- xylophone

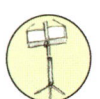

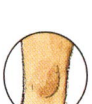

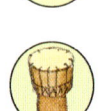

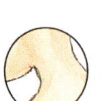

Myself
Page 4-5

- angry
- ankle
- arm
- back
- ears
- elbow
- excited
- eyes
- face
- feet
- fingers
- hair
- hand
- happy
- head
- hungry
- jealous
- knee
- leg
- mouth
- neck
- nose
- sad
- scared
- shoulders
- shy
- sick
- stomach
- teeth
- thumb
- tired
- toes
- waist
- wrist

Numbers 1-20
Page 57

- one
- two
- three
- four
- five
- six
- seven
- eight
- nine
- ten
- eleven
- twelve
- thirteen
- fourteen
- fifteen
- sixteen
- seventeen
- eighteen
- nineteen
- twenty

Opposites
Page 58-59

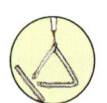

- back
- closed
- cold
- dry
- empty
- far
- fast
- front
- full
- heavy
- hot
- large
- left
- light
- long
- near

open	sandpit	pedestrian crossing	protractor	seaweed	square	stars
right	seesaw	red man	reading book	shells	star	sun
short	skip	reflector	rubber/eraser	spade	triangle	Uranus
slow	slide	road	ruler	starfish	**Space** Page 50-51	Venus
small	swing	school crossing patrol officer	string	sun lotion	comet	**Sport** Page 46-47
sour	tunnel	seat belt	writing book	waves	Earth	badminton
sweet	under	stop	**Seaside** Page 32-33	**Seasons** Page 54	Jupiter	ball
wet	up	traffic light	beach	Spring	Mars	basketball
Playground Page 34-35	**Road Safety** Page 24-25	**School Bag** Page 38-39	bucket	Summer	Mercury	bat
behind	children crossing	compass	crab	Autumn/Fall	moon	cricket
climbing frame	cycle helmet	crayon	deckchair	Winter	Neptune	cycling
down	go	felt tip pen	lifeguard	Monsoon	Pluto	football
in	green man	folder	pebbles	**Shapes** Page 56	rocket	hockey
in front	lights	maths book	rock pool	circle	Saturn	ice skates
out	listen	money	sand	cone	shooting star	netball
over	look	pencil	sandcastle	oval	Solar system	racquet
roundabout	pavement	pencil sharpener	sea	rectangle	spaceship	roller skates

63

rugby	cinema	chess	boat	cucumber	foggy	crocodile
skateboard	fire station	dice	bus	garlic	hail	dolphin
swimming	garage	doll	car	lettuce	icy	elephant
tennis	hospital	doll's house	caravan	mushroom	lightning	giraffe

Telling the Time Page 55

	library	kite	coach	onion	rainbow	hippopotamus
clock	park	marbles	helicopter	peas	rainy	lion
day	police station	playing cards	lorry/truck	pepper/capsicum	snowy	monkey
evening	school	puppet	motorbike	potato	stormy	panda bear
half past	shops/stores	puzzle	rickshaw	pumpkin/squash	sunny	penguin
morning	sports centre	skipping rope	ship	radish	thunder	shark
night	supermarket	spinning top	train	sweetcorn	windy	snake
quarter past	train station	teddy bear	tram	tomato	**Wild Animals** Page 30-31	tiger
quarter to	**Toys and Games** Page 44-45	train set	**Vegetables** Page 14-15	**Weather** Page 52-53	bear	whale
watch	balloon	toy car	beans	cloudy	camel	zebra

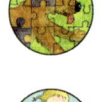

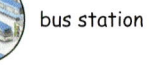

Town Page 20-21

	beads	**Transport** Page 26-27	broccoli	
bus station	board game	aeroplane	carrot	
car park	building blocks	bicycle	cauliflower	

64